LOHENGRIN

Opera in Three Acts

by

Richard Wagner

English Version by
STEWART ROBB

Ed. 2564

G. SCHIRMER, Inc.

DISTRIBUTED BY

HAL•LEONARD®
CORPORATION
7777 W. BLUEMOUND RD. P.O. BOX 13819 MILWAUKEE, WI 53213

Note

G. SCHIRMER, Inc.

DISTRIBUTED BY

HAL•LEONARD®
CORPORATION

7777 W. BLUEMOUND RD. P.O. BOX 13819 MILWAUKEE, WI 53213

LOHENGRIN

What single first appearance is the most impressive in all opera? Many answers will come to mind: the forbidding apparition of Princess Turandot in the great square at Peking; the storm-swept onrush of Otello as he proclaims "Esultate!"; the majestic entry of Norma in the procession of Druids that precedes her "Casta Diva" . . . but great and impelling as these are, surely none among them can compare to that moment in *Lohengrin* when the Swan Knight in full armor, heralded by the cries of the spectators gathered on the banks of the river Scheldt and guided into port by his own shining triplet theme in the orchestra, appears on the wave of an incomparable crescendo of volume and intensity. So irresistible is the force of this appearance that one imagines it must have always been there, like primordial rocks and waters. When one faces facts, however, one learns that the Swan Knight found no easy way into the world. The creator of *Lohengrin* had to fight for his hero.

It was with this opera that Richard Wagner drew nourishment for the last time from conventional roots and leapt toward that uncharted soil from which he was to produce the *Ring, Tristan* and *Parsifal*. By the time he reached, *Lohengrin* (1848), the problems posed by the earlier *Flying Dutchman* (1843) and *Tannhäuser* (1845) — their new harmonic and orchestral language, their bold use of musical imagery — had already been solved and the results added to the composer's craft. *Lohengrin*, in effect, stood at the end of a coastal road in Wagner's life that was to turn sharp left and up steeply toward the heights.

Wagner must have been a trial to his contemporaries. One of the leading conductors at the Royal Saxon Opera House in Dresden, he directed there not only a widely ranging repertoire of classics but also the first three of his works — *Rienzi, Flying Dutchman* and *Tannhäuser* — to win European fame. They had all been given their premiere in this theater, and it was supposed by the Saxon authorities that a certain gratitude was accruing from the composer. They had miscalculated. Aside from writing controversial new operas of his own, Wagner was imbued with the idea of reforming the theater's administration. This was disturbing to the powers in charge and they refused, in 1848, to produce Wagner's *Lohengrin*, recently completed. To add fuel to the fire, so that it became a roaring blaze, the composer had aligned himself with the political forces who took part in the chain of revolutions breaking out all over Europe. He was proscribed by the Saxon government and, in May, 1849, escaped from Dresden.

One of the great Romantics in music who had made contact with Wagner earlier in his career and who from the time of *Lohengrin* was to exercise an important sway was Franz Liszt. This remarkable man, idolized excessively while he lived and denigrated with an equal lack of perception after his death, not only scaled the heights as a master pianist; he was also a composer of strong originality (for his influence on Wagner's *Tristan,* examine the opening pages of the *Faust* Symphony) and an impresario of enormous idealism, introducing at the Court theater in Weimar — where he held forth as conductor — symphonic and operatic works by many of the gifted men of his time. To complete his association with Wagner, Liszt became, later in life, the Saxon composer's father-in-law through his celebrated daughter, Cosima. The thread of this story — Wagner and Liszt — takes us back now to April 21, 1850 when the political exile wrote despairingly from Paris to the celebrity at Weimar pleading that *Lohengrin,* which had gone unheard for two years since its completion, be produced at Liszt's Court theater. The answer came at once: the opera was to be given in August of the same year. From the standpoint of size and equipment, the house at Weimar could not have been an ideal place for so large-scale an opera; but the work was presented and had a success. Wagner himself, for political reasons, was unable to attend a performance of *Lohengrin* anywhere until nine years later; and then, after hearing his work for the first time, is said to have remarked, "Too much brass!"

The opera was not long in winning popularity. By 1858 it had reached Munich and Vienna; in 1859, Berlin and Dresden. From the 1870's date its first important performances outside Germany, notably in Bologna, London and New York. The lyricism of much of its music, combined with an over-all feeling for theatrical spectacle and grand ensembles in the tradition of Meyerbeer (much as Wagner hated and denounced that unfortunate composer) sold it at once to audiences who bought the Wedding March and ignored the opera's thornier aspects. *Lohengrin,* when approached in depth, comes off as not an easy work. The second-act night scene between Ortrud and Telramund is full of the dramatic turbulence that marks the later Wagner: darting interplay between voice and orchestra, radical key shifts and still stranger instrumental coloring, with emphasis on the darkling resources of English horn and bass clarinet. Thus, this score brought problems to the opera-goer of the 1880's who solved them by listening to what he wanted to hear, turning away from the more unsettling moments . . . while it troubles, for obverse reasons, the fan of today who hails the vitality of Ortrud's music and closes his ears to some mildewed other pages.

Great Lohengrins of the past have included Jean de Reszke, Lauritz Melchior, René Maison; great Ortruds — Ernestine Schumann-Heink, Karin Branzell, Maria Olczewska, Gertrude Kappel; great Elsas — Lillian Nordica, Elisabeth Rethberg and Lotte Lehmann.

The literary background of *Lohengrin* is bound up in medieval sources which gave rise not only to this opera but also to *Tannhäuser* and *Parsifal.* Wagner, in reading a German epic poem, "Der Wartburgkrieg" ("The Contest of Song at the Wartburg") that was to furnish much of the background material for *Tannhäuser,* came upon the figure of Wolfram von Eschenbach, the famous minstrel poet, embroidered as a character into the story. Direct research into the real-life writings of von Eschenbach brought Wagner under the spell of that writer and of his epic, "Parzival".

The legends of King Arthur's Court link Parzival for us with Perceval, whose deeds of valor were performed in company with the brave Gawain (reference is made to Gawain in Act I of Wagner's *Parsifal*, when the knight — summoned by the ailing Amfortas — fails to appear). Filling out Arthurean legend and the poem of Wolfram von Eschenbach is the epic by Chrêtien de Troyes, "Li Conte del Graal", marked — according to modern scholarship — by Persian influences. Further points of origin include the Grail legend, common to many lands; the Germanic myth of the Swan Knight, sent by Heaven to rescue the innocent in distress; and, for the plot of *Lohengrin,* a slice of history: the third decade of the tenth century A. D., with King Henry I of Saxony (Henry the Fowler), one of the principals in the drama, set to lead his forces against the invading Hungarian foe.

Out of these intermingled sources, plus Wagner's own powers of invention, were to arise *Lohengrin* and, later, *Parsifal.* The two works have much in their story line that is obviously shared: the all-pervading atmosphere of the Grail; the father-son relationship of Parsifal and Lohengrin (whose mother — according to legend — was a princess named Kondwiramur); the swan, shot in its flight by Parsifal shortly before his first entrance, and the other — more famous — bird which guides Lohengrin down the river Scheldt to Antwerp (both swans are identified by the same musical theme); the divulging of the hero's name quite late in the day (we never know the guileless fool as Parsifal until the second act of the opera, nor the Swan Knight as Lohengrin until shortly before the final curtain falls); the almost total silence of the volcanic Ortrud in the first act of *Lohengrin* and of the amazing Kundry in the last portion of *Parsifal;* and, underlying all else, the urgency of the struggle between good and evil. With *Parsifal,* at the end of Wagner's career, came compassion and an understanding of the self-induced wound suffered by those who sin. Amfortas and Kundry, in conflict and in concert, are the centers of this morality play. In *Lohengrin,* an earlier and more primitive work, the battle lines are drawn with greater harshness, with a surprising victory (no doubt an involuntary concession by Wagner at this point in his career) by the forces of evil.

The musical interest stays, for the most part, on a high plane. Thematic development in the orchestra — begun so distinctively in *The Flying Dutchman* and *Tannhäuser* — is here carried to the climax of its early use in the scores of Wagner. The *Ring* is still a giant step away . . . but the materials with which to bridge this step are already at hand.

PERFORMING NOTES

There are few standard cuts in *Lohengrin*: none at all in the first act; a brief omission in the second act of a slow-moving ensemble (from page 228, change of key to three flats, in the Schirmer piano-vocal score, to page 244, penultimate measure); and, in the final scene, a considerable cut for Lohengrin with chorus from Page 316, measure 10, to page 330, measure 2. In Act II, Ortrud's great monologue, "Entweihte Götter!" (page 142, Molto Allegro, to page 145, measure 9) is taken down a semitone when sung by mezzo-soprano. The transposition to F major begins one measure before Ortrud's vocal entry; and the old tonality is regained in the measure of Elsa's entry, with the orchestra suddenly returning to F-sharp major. When the rôle is taken by a dramatic soprano, Wagner's original notation is strictly followed.

For best effect in performance, the stage band should be retained, in addition to the large wind and brass section in the pit — with, needless to say, a sufficient body of compensating strings. Any opera company lacking the material resources with which to undertake *Lohengrin* would do best to let it alone. Had this frame of mind prevailed in 1850, there would, it is true, have been no world premiere in Liszt's modest theater at Weimar. Times, however, have changed and the greatest stages of the world are now available to Wagner. Full strength is indicated.

ROBERT LAWRENCE

THE STORY

ACT I. King Henry the Fowler, visiting tenth-century Antwerp to raise an army, holds court under an oak tree on the banks fo the river Scheldt. He calls on the regent, Frederick of Telramund, to explain why the duchy of Brabant is torn by strife and disorder. Telramund accuses his ward, Elsa, sister to the vanished heir of Brabant, of murdering her brother; convinced of her guilt, he gave up his right to Elsa's hand and married Ortrud instead. Elsa is summoned to defend herself and describes the vision in which she has beheld a knight in shining armor, who will champion her cause and whom she will wed. Twice the herald calls on him to step forward, but only after Elsa has added her prayer does Lohengrin appear, drawn up the river in a boat by a swan, to which he bids a sad farewell. The knight, greeted by Elsa as her champion, betroths himself to her on condition that she shall never ask his name or whence he comes. If she does so, he must leave. On her assent, King Henry invokes divine guidance, whereupon Lohengrin proceeds to defeat Telramund in single combat and thus to establish Elsa's innocence. She falls joyously into her savior's arms and the pair are borne off in triumph.

ACT II. Huddling before dawn in the castle courtyard, the ambitious Ortrud spurs Telramund on to assail Lohengrin's power while she herself works on Elsa's curiosity. No sooner has Elsa appeared on the balcony and voiced her serenity to the breezes than Ortrud, appealing to pagan gods for help, attempts to sow distrust in the mind of the bride. In reply Elsa urges the unhappy woman to have faith and proffers friendship, which Ortrud resolves to turn to her own use. The two enter the castle as dawn breaks and the nobles assemble, eagerly anticipating the day's events. Telramund, banned as a traitor, furtively persuades four of his henchmen to side with him against Lohengrin, whom the herald proclaims Guardian of Brabant. The courtiers welcome Elsa as she and her bridal retinue enter in stately procession. At the steps of the cathedral, first Ortrud and then Telramund attempt to break up the wedding, she by suggesting that the unknown knight is an impostor and he by accusing Lohengrin of sorcery. The crowd stirs uneasily. Although Elsa assures her champion that she believes in him, the poison of doubt begins to work. King Henry leads the couple into church.

ACT III. After a brilliant orchestral introduction, the curtain rises on the bridal chamber, to which Elsa is escorted by her maidens in the well-known Wedding Chorus. The King leads in Lohengrin, gives his blessing to the pair and retires with the company. As their voices die away, the knight draws Elsa to him and joins her in a rapturous duet, which gives way to growing anxiety on the part of the bride, when in hysterical despair, she begs to know his name and whence he comes. Suddenly Telramund and the four treacherous nobles burst upon the scene. With a cry Elsa hands Lohengrin his sword, with which the knight strikes his enemy lifeless. Ordering the nobles to bear Telramund's body to the King, he sadly tells Elsa that he will meet her there and answer her questions.

Again on the banks of the Scheldt, King Henry holds assembly in preparation for marching against the foe. Telramund's bier is brought in, followed by Elsa, scarcely able to walk, and Lohengrin, who declares that he cannot lead them, reveals that he has slain the traitor in self-defense, and explains his parentage and the distant country to which he now must return. His home is the temple of the Holy Grail at Monsalvat; Parsifal is his father and Lohengrin his name. Prophesying victory for the King's forces, the knight sorrowfully bids Elsa farewell and turn to his faithful swan, which has meanwhile neared the shore. Ortrud rushes in, exulting in Elsa's betrayal of the one man who could have broken the evil spell that transformed into a swan her lost brother Gottfried. But as Lohengrin prays, a dove descends and hovers over the swan, which vanishes; Gottfried steps forth in its place. The dove draws the boat away with Lohengrin as Elsa expires in her brother's arms.

Courtesy of Opera News

CAST OF CHARACTERS

LOHENGRIN, Knight of the Holy Grail . . . . Tenor

HENRY I., King of Germany . . . . Bass

FREDERICK TELRAMUND, a Noble of Brabant . . . . Baritone

THE ROYAL HERALD . . . . Bass

GOTTFRIED, Elsa's brother . . . . Mute

FOUR NOBLES OF BRABANT . . . . Tenors and Basses

ELSA OF BRABANT . . . . Soprano

ORTRUD, wife of Telramund . . . . Mezzo-Soprano

FOUR PAGES . . . . Sopranos and Altos

Chorus of Saxon and Brabantian Nobles, Ladies, Pages, etc.

Antwerp, First Half of the 10th Century.

SYNOPSIS OF SCENES

INDEX

x

Lohengrin.

PRELUDE.

English Version by
STEWART ROBB

RICHARD **WAGNER**.

3 Flutes, 2 Oboes, 1 Corno inglese, 2 Clarinets in A, 1 Bass Clarinet, 3 Bassoons, Horns in E & D
3 Trumpets in D, 3 Trombones, Tuba, Kettle-Drums in A & E, Cymbals, 4 Solo Violins, & Strings.

Adagio.

Piano.

45611cx

Printed in U.S.A.

Act I.

First Scene.

2 Flutes, 2 Oboes, 2 Clarinets in B♭, 3 Bassoons, Horns in E & D, 3 Trumpets in F, 3 Trombones, Tuba, Kettle-Drums in C, & Strings.

Rather fast.

Piano.

(Here the curtain rises.— A meadow on the banks of the Scheldt near Antwerp. King Henry under the Oak of Justice, surrounded by the Counts and Nobles of the Saxon arrière-ban.)

(Opposite to them the Counts and Nobles of Brabant, headed by Frederick of Telramund, with Ortrud by his side. The Herald advances from the party of the King to the centre of the stage; on a sign from him, four royal Trumpeters blow a summons.)

4 Tpts. on the stage.

Herald.

Hört! Gra-fen, Ed-le, Frei-e von Bra-
Hark! Princ-es, no-bles, free-men of Bra-

Orchestra.

ich euch erst der Drangsal Kun - de sa - gen, die deut-sches Land so
I re - late to you the dire dis - as - ters Which of - ten from the

oft aus O - sten traf? In fern - ster Mark hiesst Weib und Kind ihr
East have swept our land? How on our fron - tiers pray our wives and

be - ten: „Herr Gott, be - wahr' uns vor der Un-garn Wuth!" Doch
chil - dren: "Lord God, pro - tect us from Hun-gar - ian rage!" Yet

fp *Wind.* *fp* *fp* *fp* *fp* Str.

mir, des Reiches Haupt, musst' es ge - zie-men, solch wil-der Schmach ein En - de zu er -
I, as king-dom's head, knew it my du - ty To put an end to shame so wild and

sin - nen; als Kam - pfes Preis ge - wann ich Frie - den auf neun
woe - ful; As prize of war I won the peace For full nine

Allegro. *3*

in time.

Jahr,' ihn nützt' ich zu des Rei - ches Wehr; be - schirm - te
years, and used the time to arm the land. I for - ti -

Tpts. 3

Städt' und Bur - gen liess ich bau'n, den Heer - bann über - te ich zum
fied the towns and raised up tow'rs, And now I sum - mon you to

Wind.

Wi - derstand. Zu End' ist nun die Frist, der Zins ver -
take up arms. The term is at an end, our trib - ute

Tpts.

sagt, mit wil - dem Drohen rüs - tet sich der Feind.
too. Our foe pre-pares with wild and rumbling threats.

Allegro. *(with much warmth.)*

Nun ist es Zeit, des Rei - ches Ehr' zu
Now it is time to guard our na - tion's

Ehr'!
land!

Ehr'!
land!

The King (slower, freely declaimed.)

Komm' ich zu euch nun, Männer von Brabant, zur Hee-res-folg' nach Mainz euch zu ent-
Men of Bra - bant, I've come to you this day To sum-mon you to Mentz, with all your

bie-ten, wie muss mit Schmerz und Kla-gen ich er-seh'n, dass oh-ne
forc-es. Great are my pain and woe to see you thus, Dwell-ing in

Für-sten ihr in Zwie-tracht lebt! Ver-wir-rung, wil-de
dis-cord since you lack a lord. Con-fu-sion, fu-rious

Feh-de wird mir kund; drum ruf' ich dich, Friedrich von Tel-ra-mund! Ich
feud-ing meet me here. So let me hear, Fred-rick of Tel-ra-mund! I

45611

ken - ne dich als al - ler Tu - gend Preis, jetzt re - de, dass der Drangsal Grund ich
know you as a man of might-y worth, Now tell me what it is that brought this

Frederick (with solemnity.)

weiss. Dank, König, dir, dass du zu rich-ten kamst!
strife. Thanks, no - ble king, for hav-ing come to judge!

Maestoso. *Wind.* *Str.*

Die Wahr-heit künd' ich, Un-treu' ist mir fremd!
The truth is o - pen, false-hood is my foe!

Zum Ster - ben kam der Her - zog von Bra - bant,
When death ap-proached our great duke of Bra - bant,
und mei - nem
He chose to

Schutz empfahl er sei - ne Kin - der, El-sa, die Jungfrau, und Gottfried, den
make me guard-ian of his chil - dren, El-sa, the maid-en, and Gott-fried, her

Bru- der, da sie, von un- ge- fähr von ihm ver- irrt, bald sei- ne Spur, so
broth- er, Whom she by some strange ac- ci- dent had lost, And nev- er more —so

sprach sie, nicht mehr fand.
said she— found his trace.

Agitato.

Frucht - - los war all' Be- müh'n— um den Ver- lor- 'nen;
Fruit - - less was all our la- - bor for the lost one.

als ich mit Dro- hen nun in El- sa drang, da liess in bleichem Zagen und Er-
When I ac- cused the girl and ut- tered threats, Her sud- den pal- lor, cou- pled with her

be- ben der grässlichen Schuld Bekenntniss sie uns seh'n.
trem- bling, Were proof of the hor- rid mis- deed she had done.

Fast.

45611

Kla - ge wi - der El - sa von Bra - bant:
raise com-plaint of El - sa of Bra - bant:
des
She

ff Hns. *fp Trombs.* *ff Str.*

Bru - der-mor-des zeih' ich sie.
slew her broth-er: this I charge.
Diess
I

ff Hns. *fp Trombs.* *ff Str.*

Land doch sprech' ich für mich an mit Recht,
now claim that this land is mine by right,
da ich der
Since I am

ff

Nächste von des Her-zogs Blut, mein Weib da-zu aus dem Ge-
next the no-ble count by blood. My wife, be-sides, is of the

f *p* *f*

schlecht, das einst auch die - sen Landen sei - ne Für - sten gab.
race that once Brought forth the might-y lords who ruled our realm.

f *Trombs.* *D. Bass.* *ff*

The King.

Welch'fürch-ter-li-che Kla-ge sprichst du aus!
A fright-ful ac-cu-sa-tion you have brought!

kund!
dread!

kund!
dread!

kund!
dread!

Tnr.
p
Bssn.

Frederick. (becoming more vehement.)

Wie wä-re mög-lich sol-che gro-sse Schuld? O Herr,
Is guilt so wick-ed e-ven pos-si-ble? O King,

traum-se-lig ist die eit-le Magd, die mei-ne Hand voll
dream-fud-dled is that fool-ish maid, Who proud-ly drew a-

fp

Hochmuth von sich stiess. Ge - hei - mer Buhl-schaft klag' ich drum sie an: sie
way her hand from mine. I now ac - cuse her, too, of se - cret love. She

ly becoming more and more excited.)

wähn - te wohl, wenn sie des Bru - ders le - dig, dann könn - te sie als
dreamed, per-haps, if she re-moved her broth-er, Then she could rule as

Her - rin von Bra - bant mit Recht dem Lehnsmann ih - re Hand ver -
mis - tress of Bra - bant And there - fore right - ly cast a - side her

(The King, with a grave gesture,
reproves Frederick's vehemence.)

weh - ren, und of - fen des ge - hei - men Buh - len pfle - gen.
liege-man, To o - pen-ly en - joy her se - cret lov - er.

Molto Allegro.

cresc.

The King.

Ruft die Be-klag - te her! (with great solemnity.) Be - gin - nen
Call the ac-cused one here! For judg - ment

45611

Herald.

Scene II.

Elsa enters; she remains awhile at back, then very slowly and timidly advances to the front (centre.) The ladies of her train remain during the first part of the scene in the extreme background, on the outer edge of the judgment-circle.

3 Flutes, 2 Oboes, 1 Corno Inglese, 2 Cls. in B♭, Bass Cl., 3 Bassoons, Horns in F and E flat, 3 Trumpets in E flat, 3 Trombones, Tuba, Kettle-Drums, Strings and Harp.

(raising her voice.)

Trö - stung er mir ein: des___ Rit - ters will ich
sor - row set me free. I___ now a-wait his

(rapturously)

wah - ren, er soll mein Strei - ter sein! Er___
com - ing, He is my knight to be! He

rit.

___ soll mein Strei-ter sein!
___ is my knight to be!

All the Men. (much moved.)

Be - wah - re
May heav'n - ly

Wind & Hp.

uns des___ Him - mels___ Huld, dass
grace pour down its___ light, That

The King.

(more animatedly.)

Fried-rich, du eh-ren-wer-ther Mann, be-den-ke wohl, wen klagst du
Fred-rick, most hon-or-wor-thy man, Be-think you well whom you ac-

Schuld!
guilt.

accel.

Frederick.

an? Mich ir-ret nicht ihr träu-me-ri-scher
cuse. Her dream-y mood does not mis-lead my

Più vivo.

gradually animating the time.

(with growing excitement.)

Muth; ihr hört, sie schwärmt_____ von ei-nem Buh-len! Wes' ich sie
mind. You hear, she raves_____ a-bout a lov-er! My charge is

zeih', des' hab' ich si - chern Grund: glaub-wür-dig ward ihr Frevel mir be -
true: I stand on sol - id ground. Wit - ness most wor-thy has re-vealed her

zeugt. Doch eu - rem Zwei-fel durch ein Zeug - niss weh-ren, das___
crime. Yet to de-fend my words by such a wit-ness Would___

___stünde wahr-lich ü - bel mei-nem Stoltz! Hier
___ on -ly be ab-hor-rent to my pride! Here

steh' ich, hier mein Schwert! Wer wagt von euch zu streiten
stand I, here my sword! Who here will dare con-tend a-

richt!   Zum   Got - tes-ge - richt!   Wohl -
God!   The   judg - ment of   God!   A -

Tur. K. Dr.   *cresc.*

(The King draws his sword and strikes it before him into the earth.)

The King.

Dich   frag'   ich,
I   ask   you,

an!   *Str.*
greed!

Tromb. & Tb.

Fried - rich, Graf   von   Tel - ra-mund!   Willst   du   durch Kampf auf
Fred - rick, Count   of   Tel - ra-mund!   Will   you   en - gage   in

Trombs.

Le - ben und auf Tod   im   Got - - tes - ge - richt ver -
life   and death en - coun - ter   Now,   and en - trust   your

dim.

Kr. D.

(The Herald advances with the four Trumpeters, whom he places towards the four points of the compass at the outer edge of the judgment-circle, where they blow the summons.)

Elsa (drawing nearer to the King.)

Sei - te bleibt das Recht! Mein lie - ber Kö - nig, lass dich
right is on my side. My gra-cious sov'reign, let me

steht es schlecht!
goes quite ill!

Ob.

Wind.

(ingenuously.)

bit - ten, noch ei - nen Ruf an mei - nen Rit-ter! Wohl weilt er
beg you Yet one more cry to reach my cham-pion! He may be

The King (to the Herald.)

fern und hört' ihn nicht. Noch ein - - mal ru - fe zum Ge-
far and hear it not. Yet one _____ more time to call him

accel.

cresc.

Str.

più f

(On a sign from the Herald, the Trumpeters again
blow towards the four points of the compass.)

richt!
here!

ff

Herald.

Wer hier im
He who in

Got-tes-kampf zu strei-ten kam für El-sa von Bra-bant, der tre-te
sight of God would take the sword For El-sa of Bra-bant, let him ap-

vor! Der tre-te vor!
pear! Let him ap-pear!

All the Men.

In dü-st'rem Schwei-gen rich-tet
In gloom-y si-lence God does

Gott!
judge!

Molto agitato.

(Elsa sinks in fervent prayer on her knees; her ladies, concerned for her, come nearer to the front.) **Elsa.**

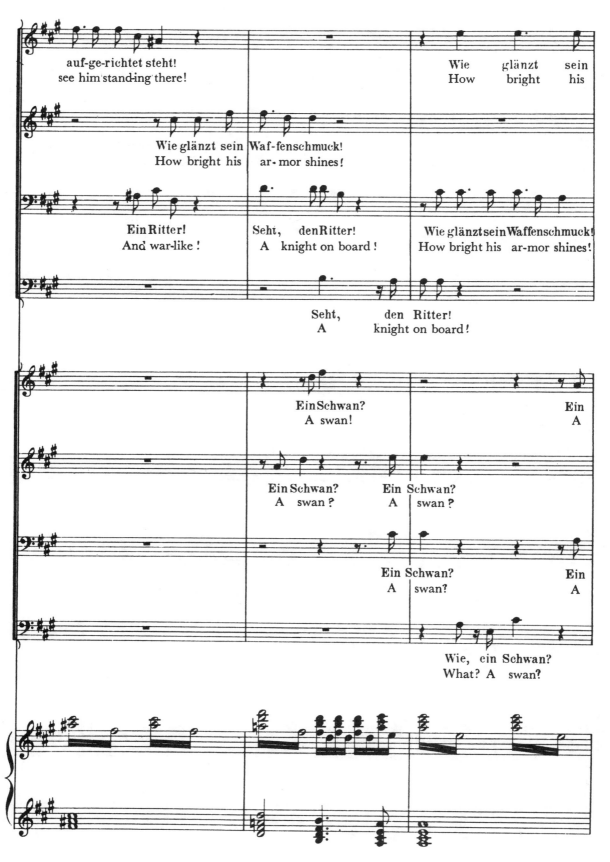

(Here a bend of the river conceals Lohengrin from view, *R. H.*; the performers, however, can see him from the stage.)

Ket - te zieht der Schwan! An ei - ner gold' - nen Ket - te zieht der
by a chain of gold! The swan con-veys him by a chain of

an! O seht! An ei - ner gold' - nen Ket - te zieht der
shore! O see! The swan con-veys him by a chain of

an! Seht, immer nä - her kommt zum U - fer er her -
shore! Look, he is draw - ing near and now he's gained the

Seht, immer nä - her kommt zum U - fer er her -
Look, he is draw - ing near and now he's gained the

(The last ones now hasten to the back of the stage, the front
of which is occupied only by the King, Elsa, Frederick, Ortrud and the Ladies.)

dort! dort!
there! there!

dort! dort!
there! there!

dort! dort!
there! there!

Wun - - der!
won - - der!

Vls.

f

Cello & Bass.

(The King, from his raised seat, sees all that passes; Frederick and Ortrud are petrified with surprise and dread; Elsa, who has listened to the exclamations of the men with growing transports, remains in her place in the centre of the stage, not daring to look around.)

(All here turn their eyes expectantly to the back of the stage.)

Scene III.

(Here the skiff, drawn by the swan, reaches the shore in the centre at the back of the stage; Lohengrin, in a silver coat of mail, with a shining helmet, his shield at his back, a little golden horn at his side, stands within it, leaning on his sword. Frederick gazes on Lohengrin in speechless amazement. Ortrud, who during the preceding had preserved a cold and haughty bearing, is seized by terrible consternation at the sight of the swan. All deferentially bare their heads.)

1 Piccolo, 2 Flutes, 3 Oboes, 3 Cls. in A, 3 Bassoons, Horns in E and A, 3 Trumpets in E, 3 Trombones, Bass Tuba, Kettle-Drum in A and E, Cymbals and Strings.

toward the swan.)

lie - ber Schwan! Zieh' durch die wei - te Fluth zu-rück da - hin, wo-her mich
lov - ed swan! Sail back the wa - t'ry ways— a - gain From whence your skiff has

Vls.

pp

trug dein Kahn, kehr' wie-der nur zu un - serm Glück! Drum sei ge - treu dein
car-ried me. Come once a-gain when for - tune smiles. Thus hold your faith to

(The swan slowly turns the skiff and swims back on the stream; Lohengrin sorrowfully looks after it for some time.)

Dienst ge-than! Leb' wohl! Leb' wohl! mein lie - ber Schwan!
serv - ice done. Fare-well, fare-well, be - lov - ed swan!

Ob. Cl. Cor. Ingl.
pp

Chorus.

SOPR. (as delicately as possible.)

ALTO. *pp*

Wie fasst uns se - lig sü - sses Grauen, welch' hol - de
We feel an awe — of bless-ed sweet-ness! What gra - cious

1st TENOR. (in falsetto.) *pp*
Wie fasst uns se - lig sü - sses Grauen, welch' hol - de
We feel an awe — of bless-ed sweet-ness! What gra - cious

2nd TENOR. *pp*
Wie fasst uns se - lig Grau - en!
We feel an awe - some sweet - ness!

1st BASS. *pp*
Wie fasst uns se-lig Grau - en, was
We feel an awe-some sweet - ness! What

2nd BASS. *pp*
Wie fasst uns se - lig Grau - en, welch' hol - de
We feel an awe-some sweet - ness! What bless - ed

pp
Vls.
'Cello.

Here Lohengrin leaves the bank, and
slowly advances towards the front.

The King.

soll von die-ser Er-de nie ver-geh'n! Hab' Dank! Erkenn' ich
name Shall nev-er per-ish from the earth! Have thanks! If I do

recht die Macht, die dich in die-ses Land ge-bracht, so nahst du uns von
reck-on right The power that led you to this land, You came to us as

Lohengrin.

Gott ge-sandt? Zum Kampf für ei-ne
sent by God. I came to com-bat

Magd zu steh'n, der schwe-re Kla-ge an-ge-than, bin ich ge-sandt, nun lasst mich
for a maid To whom a heav-y harm was done. Thus was I sent. Now let me

(He draws nearer to Elsa.)

seh'n, ob ich zurecht sie tref-fe an! So sprich denn, El-sa von Bra-
see If I can tell her from the rest! So speak then, El-sa of Bra-

bant, Wenn ich zum Streiter dir er-nannt, willst du wohl oh-ne Bang' und
bant! If I am named for your de-fense, Will you then, void of fear and

(Elsa, who has remained spellbound since she perceived Lohengrin, roused by his address and

Poco più mosso. **Elsa.**

Grau'n dich meinem Schut-ze an - ver-trau'n? Mein Held, mein
doubt, Free-ly en-trust your-self to me? My knight! 'My

overwhelmed with rapturous emotion, sinks on her knees before him.)

Adagio.

Ret-ter! Nimm mich hin! Dir geb' ich Al-les, was ich bin!
he-ro! Take me hence! All, all I give you, all I am!

Lohegrin. (with great fervor.)

Wenn ich im Kam-pfe für dich sie-ge,
If I am vic-tor in this com-bat,

Elsa.

willst du, dass ich dein Gat-te sei? Wie ich zu dei-nen
Will you grant that I be your mate? Sure as I lie right

Elsa (softy, almost unconsciously.)
Lohengrin. (with
Nam' und Art! Nie, Herr, soll mir die Fra - ge kommen! El - sa!
name and race! Lord, nev - er shall I ask such ques-tion! El - sa!
pp
Strgs.
f
raised voice, very earnestly.)
(more decisively.)
Hast du mich wohl ver-nom-men? Nie sollst du mich be - fra-gen,
Say, do you un - der-stand me? You nev - er once shall ask me,
Vl.
p
f Ob.
Fl.&Cl.
Bassn.
f
noch Wissen's Sor-ge tra-gen, wo - her ich kam der Fahrt, noch wie mein Nam' und
Nor e - ven care to won-der, From whence I journeyed here, Nor what my name and
Wind
più p
Elsa (looking up to him with intense devotion.)
Art! Mein Schirm! Mein Engel! Mein Er - lö - ser, der fest an meine
race. My shield! My an-gel! My pre-serv - er, Whose heart be-lieves me
Molto tranquillo.
Wood.
Unschuld glaubt! Wie gäb' es Zwei-fels Schuld, die grö-sser, als die an
free from guilt! How could there be a doubt more guilt-y Than that which

(Elsa and Lohengrin remain for some moments embraced.)

(Lohengrin leads Elsa to the King and gives her into his care.)

Frederick, (who has been gazing fixedly and intently at Lohengrin) vehemently.

Viel lie - ber todt, als feig!
Much bet - ter dead than fear!

Welch' Zau - - bern dich auch her - ge -
What - ev - - er mag - ic led you

führt, Fremd - ling, der mir so kühn er - in
here, Stran - ger, who make so bold in

scheint, dein stol - zes Droh'n mich nim - - mer
show, Your scorn - ful threats have no ef -

rührt, da ich zu lü - - gen nie ver -
fect, Since I do not in - tend to

The King.

So tre-tet vor, zu drei für je-den Käm-pfer, und mes-set
Step for-ward, then, with three for each con-tend-ant, And meas-ure

wohl den Ring zum Strei-te ab!
well a cir-cle round the field.

(Three Saxon Nobles advance for Lohengrin, and three Brabantians for Frederick; they cross the stage with solemn strides and measure the ground for the combat; when the six have formed a complete circle they drive their spears into the ground.)

74

Herald. (in the centre of the ring.)

Nun hö-ret mich, und ach-tet wohl: den
Now hear my words and mark me well! Let

Kampf hier Kei-ner stö-ren soll! Dem
none in-trude up-on this fight! The

Ha-ge blei-bet ab-ge-wandt, denn wer nicht wahrt des Frie-dens
space en-closed is out of bounds; If an-y man dis-turbs the

Recht, der Frei-e büss' es mit der
peace, If free-man let him lose his

Hand, mit sei-nem Haup-te büss' es der Knecht!
hand, But if a churl he pays with his head!

Kraft!
own!

The King. (solemnly.)

(The King steps into the centre.)

Kraft!   own!

Mein   Herr und Gott,
My   Lord and God,

ritard. My
Lord and God,

Tutti.

ff

ff Wind.

(Here all bare their heads, and listen devoutly.)

nun ruf' ich   dich,   dass du   dem Kampf zu - ge - gen   sei'st!   Durch
I   call on   Thee,   Ask-ing Thy   pres - ence   at   our   strife!   Speak

lunga.   *Tromb. & Tpts.*

ff   *pp*

Ped. ✳

Schwer-tes   Sieg ein   Ur-theil   sprich, das   Trug   und   Wahrheit
forth Thy   sen - tence through the   sword, Let   truth   and — false-hood

p   *cresc.*   *mf*   *dim.*

klar — er-weist!   Des   Rei-nen Arm   gieb Hel-den-kraft,   des
clear - ly show.   Give   him who's pure   he - ro - ic strength From

p   *p*

Ped.   *Ped.* ✳

nun dein wahr Ge - richt;
me Thy true de - cree!

wo er kämpft, ihm Sieg' ver-schafft; ich bau - e fest auf sei - ne
when he fights, can nev - - er fail! I build my trust up-on his

zag' ich nicht! Du
have no fear! Make

nicht! Herr Gott, ver-lass mein' Eh - re nicht! Ich
name. Lord God, up-hold my hon-ored name! I

Wahr - heit klar er - weist:
false - hood stand re - vealed!

Seg - ne ihn!
Bless Thy knight!

Ein - falt ist! So kün - de
is but fol-ly! Make known to

Herr, mein Herr, drum zag' _____ ich nicht!
then, my Lord, I have _____ no fear!

Kraft, die, wo er kämpft, ihm Sieg _____ ver-schafft!
strength, Who, when he fights, can nev - - er fail.

zag' ich nicht, drum zag' _____ ich nicht!
have no fear! I have _____ no fear!

_ ver - lass mein' Eh - re nicht!
_ up - hold my hon - ored name!

nicht, Herr, mein Gott, nun zög' - re nicht!
not! Lord, my God, de - lay _____ it not!

_ mein Gott, seg - ne ihn!
_ my God, bless ne Thy knight!

_ nun zög' - - re nicht!
_ de - lay it not!

Tutti.

Vl. & Tir.

più f   ff   ff   ff

(In excitement all resume their places, the six seconds remain standing beside the spears of the enclosure, the other men form a wider circle round them; Elsa and her ladies in the foreground under the oak, beside the King. On a sign from the Herald, the Trumpeters blow the call to battle:Lohengrin and Frederick make their final preparations.)

90

(Here Lohengrin with a
mighty stroke fells Frederick to the earth.)

(Frederick tries to raise himself, stag-
gers a few steps backwards, then falls.)

45611

Lohengrin. (with the point of his sword upon Frederick's throat.) (releasing him.)

Durch Got-tes Sieg ist jetzt dein Le-ben mein: ich
Through might of God your life be-longs to me. I

ff   Str.

Andante.   Vivo.   (All the men resume

schenk' es dir!   mögst du der Reu' es   weih'n!
spare that life: use it to cleanse your   sin!

SOPRANO & ALTO.   *ff*
Sieg!
Hail!

TENOR.   *ff*
Sieg!
Hail!

BASS.   *ff*
Sieg!
Hail!

Wind   Andante.   Vivo.
p   *p*   *ff*   *Tutti.*

Ped.

their swords, and thrust them back in their scabbards. The seconds draw out the spears, and the King takes down his shield from the oak. All triumphantly rush to the centre and fill the ground where the fight took place. Elsa hastens to Lohengrin.)

Sieg!
hail!   Sieg!
hail!

Sieg!
hail!   Sieg!
hail!

94

(She sinks upon
Lohengrin's breast.)

45611

102

45611

114

hin!
now!

hin!
gone!

sein!
rich!

hin!
done!

Fahrt!
deed!

dir!
hail!

dir!
hail!

Tutti.

ff

Ped.   *

Ped.   *

(Frederick falls senseless at the feet of Ortrud. Youths raise Lohengrin upon his shield, and Elsa upon the
shield of the King, upon which several have spread their mantles; thus both are borne away amid general rejoicing.)

Ped.   * Ped.

(The curtain falls.)

*   Ped.

Ped.

End of the first Act.

45611

Act II.
First Scene.

(On the stage behind the scenes.) *2 Flutes & Piccolo, 3 Oboes, 3 Clarinets in C, 2 Bassoons, 3 Horns in D, 3 Trombones, Kettle Drum in D, Cymbals.*

(In the Orchestra.) *3 Flutes, 2 Oboes, Corno inglese, 2 Clar.s in A, Bass Clar. in A, 3 Bssns, Horns in E & D, 3 Trumpets, 3 Trombones, Bass Tuba, Kettle Drums in F♯ & C♯, & Strings.*

(The curtain rises. Scene, the citadel of Antwerp; at the back the Palas (dwelling of Knights); in the fore-ground the Kemenate (dwelling of women); r.h. the Minster. It is night. Ortrud and Frederick, both in dark, servile garments, are seated on the steps of the Minster; Frederick is musing gloomily, Ortrud gazing fixedly at the windows of the Palas, which is brightly illuminated.)

Allegro. (Festive music is heard from the Palas.)
(On the stage.)

Tempo I.

Frederick. (rising hastily.)

Er - he - be dich, Genossin meiner Schmach! Der junge
A - rouse your-self, com-pan-ion of my shame! The dawn-ing

45611

schän - de, flieht selbst der Räu - ber mich. Durch dich, durch
sul - ly, E - ven the rob - bers flee. Through you, through

dich musst' ich ver - lie - ren mein' Ehr', all' meinen Ruhm;
you, gone is my hon - or, My hon - or and my fame.

nie soll mich Lob mehr zie - ren, Schmach ist mein Hel - den - thum! Die
No more shall praise a - dorn me, Shame is my he - ro - hood! And

Acht ist mir ge - spro - chen, zer - trüm - mert liegt mein
scorn hence - forth my dow - er. In piec - es lies my

Schwert, mein Wap - pen ward zer - bro - chen, ver -
sword, My scutch - eon has been spot - ted, My

(Music sounds in the Palas.)

ff Tpts.& Tromhs.(on the stage.)

Ortrud. (without quitting her first position while Frederick rises.)

Was macht dich in so wil-der Kla-ge doch ver-
Why do you·eat your heart by mak-ing wild com-

Slower.
Wind.

p Orch.

Frederick. (with a violent gesture.)   **Ortrud.** (with quiet scorn)

geh'n? Dass mir die Waffe selbst geraubt, mit der ich dich er-schlüg'!   Friedreicher Graf von
plaints? Curst one, be-cause I e-ven lack A sword to strike you dead!   Fred-er-ick, Count of

Str.   *f*   *f.*   *p*

Wind.

Tel-ra-mund! wes-halb miss-traust du mir?
Tel-ra-mund! why this mis-trust in me?

Frederick.

Du fragst? War's nicht dein Zeugniss, deine Kunde, die mich be-
You ask? Was't not your wit-ness, your re-port, which made me ac-

herrschen in Bra-bant? Be-wogst du so mich nicht.von El-sa's Hand, der Rei-nen, ab-zu-
lord it in Bra-bant? And did you not be-guile me from the hand Of El-sa, who is

Ortrud. (with suppressed rage.)

steh'n, und dich zum Weib zu nehmen, weil du Radbod's letzter Sross! Ha, wie töd-lich du mich kränkst!
pure, to take you For my con-sort, as the last of Radbod's race? Ha, you make me death-ly sick!

Frederick. (with great animation.)
Allegro.

Dies Al - les, ja, ich sagt' und zeugt' es dir! Und machtest mich, dess' Na-me hoch-ge-
Most tru - ly, yes, all this I said and proved. You made of me, whose name was no-bly

ehrt, dess' Le - ben al-ler höchsten Tugend Preis, zu dei-ner Lü - ge
known, Whose life was count-ed fair-est vir-tue's flower, The vile ac - com - plice

Ortrud. (defiantly.) **Frederick.**

schändlichem Ge-nos-sen? Wer log? Du! Hat nicht durch sein Gericht Gott
of your shameless ly-ing. Who lied? You! That is the rea-son why God

Ortrud. (pointing to the Palas, where the lights are now extinguished.)
rü - cken? Die Schwelger streck-ten sich zur üpp'- -gen Ruh';
tice me? The rev - lers lie out-stretched in sot - - tish rest;
(Frederick draws
setz' dich zur Sei - te mir! Die Stund' ist da, wo dir mein Se - her-au-ge
Come, sit here by my side! The hour has come For my pro - phet - ic eyes to
nearer to Ortrud, and bends his ear attentively to her words.)
leuch-ten soll!
lend you light!
Str. con Sord.
pp
B. Cl.
p
Weisst du, wer die-ser
Do you know, who he
Held, den hier ein Schwan ge - zo - gen an das Land?
is, that he - ro Brought here by a mag-ic swan?
Frederick.
Nein!
No!
Ortrud.
Was gäbst du
What would you
p Cor. ingl. & Bssn.
doch, es zu er-fah-ren, wenn ich dir sag', ist er ge - zwungen zu nen - nen,
give to know a-bout him? What if I said, if one com-pels him To ut - ter
B. Cl.
p

wie sein Nam' und Art, all sei - ne Macht zu En - de ist, die müh-voll ihm ein
forth his name and birth, Then, all that might is at an end Which he had won by

Wind. Str.

Frederick.

Zau - ber leiht? Ha! Dann be - griff' ich sein Ver - bot! Nun hör'!
mag - ic art. Ha, his for - bid - ding then made sense. Now hear!

Ob. & Cl.

Ortrud.

Nie - mand hier hat Ge - walt, ihm das Ge - heim - niss zu ent - rei - ssen, als
No one here has the pow'r To wrest the se - cret from his bos - om But

Frederick.

die, der er so streng ver - bot, die Fra - ge je an ihn zu thun. So gält' es,
she, to whom he gave com - mand To nev - er seek to ques - tion him. Our need then

Ortrud.

Elsa zu ver - lei - ten, dass sie die Frag' ihm nicht er - liess'? Ha, wie begreifst du schnell und
must be to per-suade her To put the ques - tion to the knight. How fast and well you ap - pre-

molto cresc. ff p

O Weib, _____ das in der Nacht ich vor mir seh' _ be-
O wife, _____ I see be-fore _ me in the dark, If

trügst du jetzt mich noch, dann weh' dir!
you be-tray me still, then, woe's you,

Ortrud. *rallentando poco a poco.*

ff dim.

Fl., Cor. ingl. & Cl.

Weh'! Ha, wie du ra-sest! Ru-hig und be-
woe! Ha, you are rav-ing! Keep _ calm and col-

p Moderato.

son-nen! So lehr' ich dich der Ra-che sü-sse Wonnen!
lect-ed! And I will teach you sweet-est joys of venge-ance!

Str.

p Wind. pp

B.Cl. & Bssn.

(Frederick slowly seats himself beside Ortrud.)

molto cresc. ff dim. p

Trombs. & Tb.

45611

(Here the door of the Kemenate, that leads on to the balcony, opens.)

Second Scene.

Same score (Cl. & B.Cl. in B., Horns in F & C.)

(Elsa, in a white robe, appears on the balcony; she steps forward to the parapet and leans her head on her hand; Frederick and Ortrud, opposite to her, sit on the steps of the Minster.)

138

45611

Gott, was kla-gest du mich an? War ich es, die dir Leid ge-
heav'n! why make com-plaint to me? Was I the one who brought your

Ortrud.

bracht? Wie könn-test du für-wahr mir nei-den das
woe? What rea-son did you have to en-vy That

Elsa.

Glück, dass mich zum Weib erwählt der Mann,den du so gern verschmäht? All-
luck that made me cho-sen wife To one whom you so glad-ly spurned? All-

Ortrud.

güt' - ger Gott! Was soll mir das? Musst' ihn__ unsel'ger Wahn bethören,
gra - cious God! What's this to me? If he,__ mis-led by wretch-ed fan-cy,

dich Rei - ne ei-ner Schuld zu zeih'n,__ von Reu'__ ist nun sein Herz zer-rissen, zu
Thought you, the guilt-less, full of guilt, His heart__ is torn by sore re-pent-ance,The

ger, der mich so_____ be- me
-y One who blessed_____

f Wind sustain.

glückt, wenn ich das Un-glück von mir stie- sse, das sich im
so, If I re- pelled this wretch- ed wom- an, Who bows be-

p   *più p*

Stau- be vor mir bückt!_ O nim- mer! Or- trud,
fore_ me in the dust! Oh nev- er! Or- trud!

p cresc.   *fp* cresc.

Molto Allegro.

har- re mein! Ich sel- ber lass' dich zu mir ein!
Wait ____ for me! My- self will come and let you in!

f   *f* Wind.   *f*   Str.   *ff*

(She hastens back into the Kemenate; Ortrud springs
from her seat on the Minster steps in wild exultation.)

Ortrud.

Ent -
You

ff Wind.

Trombs., B. Tb. & D. Bass.

weih - - - te Göt - - ter!
gods _____ most ho - ly!

Helft jetzt mei - ner Ra - che! Be -
Help me to my venge - ance! Re -

straft _____ die Schmach, _____ die
quite _____ the shame, _____ which

hier euch an - ge - than!
here you have re - ceived!

Stärkt mich im Dienst eu - rer heil' - gen
Make me more strong in your sa - cred

glück - - lich mei - ne Ra - - - che
tram - - meled let my venge - - - ance

Fl. Ob. & Clar.

sei!
work!

Tutti.

Elsa (still outside.)

(Elsa, with two maids bearing lights, enters by the lower door.)

Or - - trud! wo bist___ du?
Or - - trud? Where are___ you?

Fl.
Wind.

Ortrud (humbly prostrating herself before Elsa.)

Hier, zu dei - nen Fü - ssen!
Here, pros-trate be - fore you!

Elsa (starting back in alarm at the sight of Ortrud.)

Hilf Gott! So muss ich dich er - blicken, die ich in
Oh God! That I should thus be - hold you, Whom once I

Stolz und Pracht nur sah! Es will das Her-
saw in splen-did pride! My heart will choke

-ze mir er-sticken, seh' ich so nie-drig dich mir
me in my bos-om Just see-ing you a-based like

(Not too fast.)

nah! Steh' auf! O, spa-re mir dein Bit-ten!
this! Get up! O, spare me all this plead-ing!

Trugst du mir Hass, ver-zieh ich dir; was du schon jetzt durch
Did you bear hate, I par-don you; What-ev-er, too, I've

mich ge-lit-ten, das, bit-te ich, ver-zeih' auch mir, das, bit-te
made you suf-fer, That, if you will, for-give me, too, That, if you

45611

Elsa (with rising pleasurable emotion.)

mich in Dan — — kes Ban — den! In Früh'n lass mich be —
me with bonds of good — ness! By ear — ly morn — ing

reit dich seh'n! Ge — schmückt mit
be pre — pared, At — tired in

präch — ti — gen Ge — wan — — den sollst du mit mir zum Mün — ster
beau — ti — ful a — dorn — — ment, We'll walk to — geth — er to the

geh'n: — Dort har — re ich des Hel — den
church. There will I wait my he — ro

mein, vor Gott sein Eh' — — ge — mahl zu
groom, To be his bride — — in sight of

(with joyous pride.)

45611

ff
slowly.
(rapturously.)
p
sein, vor Gott sein Eh' - - ge-mahl zu sein! Sein
God! To be his bride in sight of God! His
Fl.
poco allarg.
p
f
p poco rit.
Wind.
Tnr.
Eh' - ge - mahl!
hon - ored bride!
Fl. & Clar.
Str.
pp
ff
Wind sustain.
Ped.
*
Ortrud.
Wie kann ich sol - che Huld dir
How can I give such grace re -
Tnr.
dim.
p
Trombs. sustain.
Vl. & Basses pizz.
loh - nen, da macht - los ich und
pay - ment, Since I am poor and
e - lend bin? Soll ich in
pow - er - less? Though through your
Vl. divided.
p
'Cello.

Elsa (artlessly Ortrud (vehemently.)
and kindly.)   (moderating herself.)

Noth! Wie meinst du? Wohl dass ich dich war - ne, zu blind nicht dei-nem Glück zu
gret. What say you? Just at-tend my warn - ing, Do not too blind-ly trust your

Più lento.

traun; dass nicht ein Un-heil dich um - - gar-ne, lass mich für dich zur Zukunft
luck, Just so a mis-hap may not hurt you. Now let me scry your future

Elsa (shuddering inwardly.) Adagio.   Ortrud (with great mystery.)

schaun. Welch' Un-heil?   Könn-test du er-fas-sen, wie des-sen
fate. What mis-hap?   Have you nev-er won-dered How with an

Art so wun-der-sam, der nie dich mö-ge so ver-las-sen, wie er durch
art so mar-vel-ous, This man might leave you through that mag-ic, Through that same

(turns again to Ortrud full of
(Elsa turns away, seized with secret dread.) compassion.)
Più vivo.   Moderato. Elsa (Freely declaimed.)

Zau-ber zu dir kam!   Du
art where-by he came?   Poor

45611

Aermste kannst wohl nie er_mes_sen, wie zwei-fel_los mein Her_ze liebt!
wom-an, you can nev-er meas-ure How free from doubt my lov-ing heart,

Du hast wohl nie das Glück_ be-ses-sen, das sich uns nur durch Glau-be
Nor have you known the hap-pi-ness That can on-ly come to us through

Moderato, a tempo. (kindly.)

giebt? Kehr' bei mir ein! Lass'mich dich leh-ren, wie
faith. Come in with me! Let me but teach you How

süss die Won-ne rein-sterTreu'! Lass_ zu dem Glau-_ben
sweet the joy of pur-est trust! Let_ faith con-vert you

rallentando poco a poco.

dich be – keh – ren: es giebt ein Glück, es giebt ein Glück, das oh – ne
to this know-ledge. There tru – ly is a hap – pi – ness with – out re –

Molto tranquillo, ma non lento.

Reu'! Lass mich dich Ich – ren, wie
gret! Let me but teach — you How

Ortrud (aside.)

Ha! Die – ser Stolz, er soll mich leh – ren, wie ich be – käm – pfe ih – re
Ha! What a pride! I'll let it teach me How to com – bat this faith of

Molto tranquillo, ma non lento.

süss — die — Won – – ne rein – – ster Treu – e;
sweet — the — joy — of pur – – est trust! —

Treu', er — soll mich's leh – ren! Gen ihn — will ich die Waf – fen keh – ren,
hers, I'll — let it teach me A – gainst — it I will turn the weap – ons:

154

45611

Moderato.

__ in dies Haus! Voll - füh - re, Weib, was dei - ne List er - son - nen; dein
__ in that house! O wom - an, act what you have sub - tly plot - ted. I

Werk zu hemmen fühl' ich kei - ne Macht! Das Un - heil hat mit
lack the might to hin - der what you do. My down - fall was the

meinem Fall be - gon - nen, — nun stür - zet nach, die mich da - hin ge -
start of all this mis - chief. Down let them plunge who brought me to my

bracht! Nur Ei - nes seh' ich mah - nend vor mir
fall! There's on - ly one thing plain be - fore my

stehn: der Räu - ber mei - ner Eh - re soll ver -
eyes: The rob - bers of my hon - or shall be

Scene III.

Gradual daybreak. Two warders blow the Reveille from the turret, which is answered from another turret in the distance.)

Same score (3 Clarinets in A, Horns in D, Trumpets in D, Kettle Drums in A. & D,) afterward Harp.

(While the warders descend from the turret and unlock the gates, servitors of the Castle enter from various directions; they salute each other and proceed quietly on their several ways : some draw water at the well, in metal vessels, knock at the entrance of the Palas and are admitted.)

(The gates of the Pal-

as are opened again, the four Royal Trumpeters issue from them and blow the call.)

(The trumpeters reënter

the Palas; the servitors have left the stage.)

(From here the Nobles and the inhabitants of the fortress enter, some

from the city road, others from various quarters of the citadel, and in increasing number.)

164

45611

viel, gar viel!
deeds. great deeds!

viel, gar viel!
deeds, great deeds!

gar viel, gar viel!
great deeds, great deeds!

gar viel, gar viel!
great deeds, great deeds!

(The Herald comes out of the Palace preceded by the four Trumpeters. All turn in anxious expectation towards the back of the scene.)

Hns. & Bssn. Str.

Tutti.

4 Tps. on the stage.

Tps. on the stage.

The Herald. (on the elevation before the gates of the Palas.)

Poco più lento.

Des Kö-nigs Wort und Will' thu' ich euch kund; drum ach-tet
Our sov'reign's word and will now are pro-claimed. Heed well the

wohl, was euch durch mich er sagt! In Bann und Acht
words he speaks to you through me! Out-lawed and banned

— ist Fried-rich Tel-ra-mund, weil un-treu er den Got-tes-kampf ge-
— is Fred-rick Tel-ra-mund, Be-cause he knew his guilt yet dared to

wagt: wer sein noch pflegt, wer sich zu ihm ge-sellt, nach
fight. Who shel-ters him, who treats him as a friend, Will

Rei-ches Recht der-sel-ben Acht ver-fällt.
be by self-same roy-al rule con-demned.

Chorus of Men.

1st & 2nd Chorus.

4 Tpts. on the stage. (At the trumpet-call, the people forthwith resume their attentive attitude.)

The Herald.

Nun hört, was Er durch mich euch sa - gen
Now hear through me what he would have you

Poco più lento.
4 Tpts. on the stage. Orchestra.

lässt: _ heut' fei - ert er mit euch sein Hochzèit-fest; _ doch mor - gen sollt ihr
know: This day he holds with you his wed-ding feast; But on the mor-row

kampf-ge-rüs-tet nah'n, zur Hee-res-folg' dem Kö--nig un--ter-than; er selbst ver-
be in bat--tle trim, To fol-low him as sol-diers of the king, While he him-

fp

Ped. ✻ Ped.

(with warmth.)

schmäht der sü-ssen Ruh' zu pfle-gen, er führt euch an zu hehren Ruh=mes Se-
self dis-dains the balm of sweet rest To lead you forth to top most height_of glo-

cresc. *f*

✻

Molto Allegro.

(After a short while, the Herald with the four Trumpeters return into the palas.)

gen!
ry!

1st & 2nd Chorus. (with exultation.)

ff

Zum Strei -
Be read -

ff

Zum Strei -
Be read -

ff

Zum Strei -
Be read -

ff

Zum Strei -
Be read -

Molto Allegro.

accel. Str.

p Tps. molto *cresc.* *più f* *ff.* Wind.

45611

187

45611

bald will ich wohl wei-ter noch mich wa-gen, vor eu-ern
soon You'll see how far my dar-ing takes me, Quite soon your

Au-gen soll es leuch-tend ta-gen! Der euch so kühn die
eyes will see it plain as day-light! He who so bold-ly

Heerfahrt an-ge-sagt, der sei von mir des Got-tes-trugs be-
calls you forth to war, I will ac-cuse of treach-er-y to

(Four Pages issue from the door of the Kemenate upon the balcony; they gaily run down the staircase and stand before the doorway of the Palas.)

klagt!
God!

1st & 2nd Noble.

Was hör ich! Was hast du vor? Weh' dir
What say you? What will you do? Watch out,

3rd Noble.

Was hör ich! Was hast du vor? Ver-lor'-ner du,
What say you? What will you do? You ma-ni-ac,

4th Noble.

Ra-sen-der! Was hast du vor? Ver-
Blus-ter-er! What will you do? You're

(The Nobles urge Frederick towards the Minster, where they endeavor to conceal him from the populace.)

hört dich des Vol - - kes Ohr!
don't let the peo - - ple hear!

hört dich des Vol - - kes Ohr!
don't let the peo - - ple hear!

lor' - ner, hört dich das Volk!
done for if you are heard!

cresc.

(The populace, perceiving the Pages, crowd towards the front.)

poco cresc.

più cresc.

Str. & Tpts.

Four Pages. (on the terrace before the Palas.)

Macht Platz!
Make way,

Macht Platz!
make way,

stacc.

stacc.

Vl.
Wind.

für El - sa, un - sre Frau:
our La - dy El - sa comes,

die will in Gott zum Mün - ster
Up - held by God — she pass - es

(They come down the stage, opening a wide passage through the readily yielding nobles to

geh'n.
by!

the steps of the Minster, where they take their stand.)

Andante.

(Four other Pages come with measured steps from the upper door of the Kemenate, and stand on
the balcony, awaiting the train of Ladies which they are to accompany.)

Fourth Scene.

Same Score (Cl. in B♭, Hns. in E flat), except Hp.

(A long train of ladies, magnificently attired, proceeds slowly from the Kemenate, passing before the Palas (L.H.); then, returning to the front, they ascend the steps of the Minster, where the first-comers arrange themselves.)

Largo e solenne.

Here Elsa appears amid the train; the Nobles deferentially bare their heads.)

Gott hü - te ih - ren Schritt!
And ev - er guide her so!

mö - ge sie ge - lei - ten,   Gott
God di - rect her foot - -steps,   And

Ped. ✳ *Ped.* ✳

(The Nobles, who have involuntarily pressed forward
again, here make way for the Pages, who clear the
road for the train which by this time has arrived
before the Palas.)   (Here Elsa has reached

Sie naht,
She comes,

hü - te ih - ren Schritt!
ev - er guide her so!

Vl.

più p

pp   *Wind sustain.*

Ped. ✳ *Ped.* ✳   *Ped.*   ✳

the terrace of the Palas; the way is again clear, so that all can see her. She remains awhile

(From here Elsa proceeds slowly to
the front, through the path left open
by the men.)

(Here, besides the Pages, the foremost Ladies have reached the steps of the Minster, where they stand aside to let Elsa pass into the Church before them.)

(As Elsa places her foot on the second step of the Minster, Ortrud, who till now has been at the rear of the train of Ladies, hastily comes forward, and places herself on the same step, thus confronting Elsa.)

sehn? Welch' jä - her Wech - sel ist mit dir ge -
see? What sud - den change has tak - en place in
(They push Ortrud back to the centre of the stage.)

rück!
back!
Weib?
want?

3 Bssn. dim. p

Ortrud.

schehn? Weil ei - ne Stund' ich meines Werth's ver - ges - sen, glau - best
you? Though I had let my worth to be for - got - ten, Do you

p fp Ob.

Cello.

du, ich mü - sste dir nur krie - chend nah'n? _____ Mein
think that I should crawl be - fore your feet? _____ My

cresc. -

con molta forza

Leid zu rä - chen, will ich mich ver - mes - sen, was mir ge - bührt, das
woes and sor-rows cry a - loud for venge-ance! That which is due, that

f fp fp fp

Wind. Ped. Ped.

204

45611

Gott im Kampf ge-schla- - -
God my he- - -ro con- - -

-gen mein theu-rer Held den Gat- -ten
-quer Your hus-band on the field of

(to the People.)
dein? Nun sollt nach Recht ihr
arms? Now shall you all in

Al- -le sa-gen, wer
truth ___ af-firm it, Who

___ kann da nur der Rei-ne
___ stands a-lone in pu-ri-

wie wä - re sie so bald ___ ge - trübt,
I fear it would be soon ___ dis - turbed,

müsst' er des Zau - bers We - sen mel - den,
If he con-fessed that mag - ic prac - tice

durch den hier sol - che Macht er übt!
Through which deeds of such might were done!

Wagst du ihn nicht ___ dar - um zu fra - gen,
Are you a - fraid ___ to put the ques - tion?

(emphatically.)
so glau - ben Al - le wir ___ mit Recht,
If so, we all are right ___ to think,

Fifth Scene.

Same Score, afterwards Organ.

The King, Lohengrin, and the Saxon Counts and Nobles have issued from the Palas in stately procession; the commotion in front interrupts the train; the King and Lohengrin come forward hastily.

214

wagt es hier den Kir-chen-gang zu stö - ren?
dares to clam-or here be-fore the Min - ster?

The Train of the King. *ff*

Welcher Streit, den wir ver-
What's this strife that we are

fp *fp* *fp* *cresc.*

Lohengrin. (perceiving Ortrud.)   **Elsa.**

Was seh' ich! Das un - sel'-ge Weib bei dir? Mein
What is this? This un - hal-lowed one with you? My

nah-men?
hear-ing?

Wind. *Str.* *Ob.*

ff *fp* *fp* *p*

Ped. ✳ Ped. ✳

Ret - ter! Schü - - tze mich vor die-ser Frau!
cham - pion! Shel - - ter me a-gainst her wrath!

fp *f* *dim.* *fp*

(he turns to Elsa, gently.)

(Elsa, weeping, hides her face on his breast.)

Sag', El - sa, mir, vermocht'ihr Gift sie in dein Herz zu gie-ssen?
Say, El - sa, say, If she has poured her poi-son in your bos- om.

(Lohengrin, raising her and pointing to the Minster.)

Komm', lass in Freu-de dort die - se Thrä-nen flie -
Come, let us go, and there let your tears be joy-

(Lohengrin, Elsa and the King turn towards the Min-ster followed by their train, who arrange themselves in order.)

ssen!
ful!

Moderato e solenne.

(Frederick comes forward on the steps of theMinster; Frederick.
the Ladies and Pages shrink from him in terror.)

Agitato.

Kö - nig! Trug-bethörte
sov-reign! Fraud-de-lud-ed

grim - mes Un-recht ihr ge-than!
whom you've done a fright-ful wrong!

The King.

Hin-weg!
A - way!

Weich' von dannen!
Leave our pres-ence!

Weich' von dannen!
Leave our pres-ence!

Hin - weg!
A - way!

Weich' von dannen!
Leave our pres-ence!

cresc.

Str.

piùf

K.Dr.

Ped.

Got - tes Ge - richt, es ward ent - ehrt, be - tro - gen! Durch ei - nes Zaub'rers
Judg - ment of God has been be - trayed by false-hood, A false-hood spun by

Trombs.&Tpts.

ffp

ff

ff

Ped.

Frederick (with a terrible effort to make himself heard, fixes his gaze on Lohengrin only, without noticing the others).

Den dort im Glanz ich vor mir
This shin - ing knight I see be -

(The throng shrinks back from Frederick; all listen attentively.)

se - he, den kla-ge ich des Zau - bers an! Wie
fore me, I here ac-cuse of mag - ic art! As

Staub vor Got-tes Hauch ver - we - he die Macht, die er durch List ge -
dust by breath of God is scat - tered, So shall his might be blown a -

wann! Wie schlecht ihr des Ge-rich - tes wahr - tet,
way! How bad - ly did you hon - or judg - ment

das doch die Eh - re mir be - nahm, da ei - ne
Who took the hon - or from my name By spar - ing

Wer ist er, der an's Land geschwommen, ge - zo - gen von ei- nem wil-den
Who is he, that most might-y man, Whom a wild swan has drawn here in a

Schwan?
boat?

Wem sol - che Zau-ber-thie-re frommen, des' Rein-heit ach-te ich für
And since he us - es mag - ic crea-tures, I doubt if he's an hon - est

Wahn!
man!

Nun soll der Klag' er
Now shall he face the

Re - de steh'n;
charge I make:

ver-mag er's, so geschah mir
If an-swered, he may prove his

Animato.

Recht,
cause;

wo nicht,___ so sol-let ihr er-
If not,___ why then it will be

seh'n,
plain

um sei - ne Rei - ne steh'___ es
His truth and hon - or look___ quite

Allegro. (all look disturbed and expectantly towards Lohengrin.)

schlecht!
bad!

Chorus of Men.

Welch' har - te
A bit - ter

Welch' har - - te
A bit - - ter

Welch' har - te Kla - - gen!
A bit - ter chal - - lenge!

Allegro.

(Lohengrin checks himself, seeing with dismay, as he turns towards Elsa, that **her bosom is** heaving convulsively and her eyes fixed in wild inward commotion.)

230

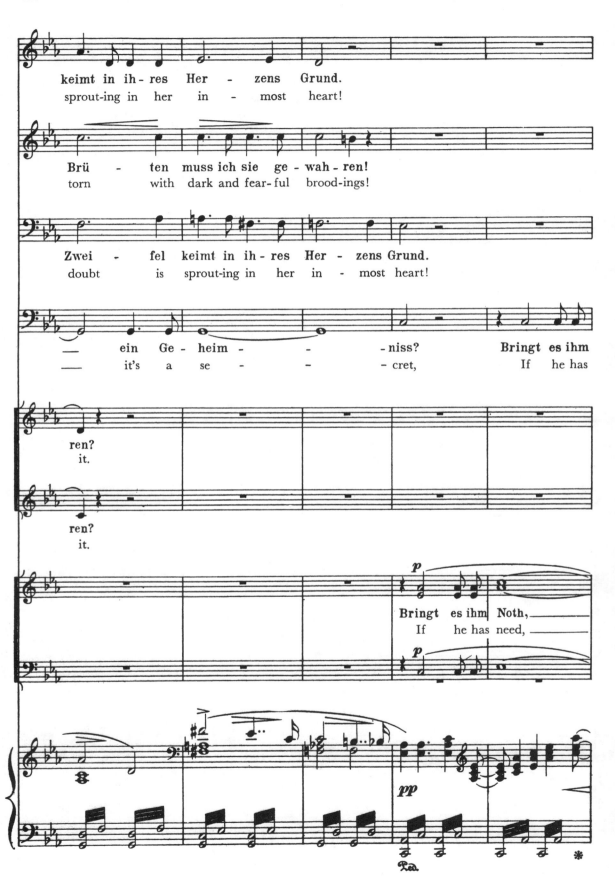

45611

236

Wüsst' ich sein Loos, wüsst' ich sein Loos!
But if I knew, but if I knew!

Er ist be-siegt, wird ihm die Fra - ge _ kund,
He will be lost if he but make re - ply,

O Him - mel, schir - me sie!
O heav - en! Guard _ her heart!

Fra - ge kund, wird ihm die Fra - ge
ply to her, If he but make re -

durch sei - ne That al - lein!
His deed a - lone gave proof!

treu sein Mund!
lock his lips!

Wir
We'll

più p

Vl.

molto cresc.

euch soll der Glau - - - be nicht ge-reu - en,
You nev - er shall _____ re-gret be-liev - ing,

dir in Treu - en, dass hehr dein Nam', auch wenn er
name in hon - or! Your name most high, al-though we

glau - ben dir in Treu - en, dass hehr dein Nam', auch
hold your name in hon - or! Your name most high,

wir glau - ben dir in Treu - en!
We hold your name in hon - or!

Reich
Give

Reich'
Give

werd' euch mein Nam' und Art _____ auch nie ge - nannt.
Al - though my name and state _____ must stay un - known!

(Frederick approaches close to Elsa, who stands, plunged in
thought, apart in the foreground.)

Frederick (in a low voice, inter-
posing vehemently.)

Vertrau - e mir!
Just take my word!

nicht genannt. Reich' uns die Hand, reich' uns die Hand!
know it not. Give us your hand! Give us your hand!

wenn er nicht ge - nannt! Reich' uns die Hand!
though we know it not. Give us your hand!
uns die Hand,
us your hand!

Reich' uns die Hand, reich' uns die Hand!
Give us your hand! Give us your hand!

uns die Hand, reich' _____ uns die Hand!
us your hand! Give _____ us your hand!

Wind.

cresc.

Tr. & Cello.

Lohengrin (stepping

Nacht,__ rufst du, ohn' Scha - den ist es schnell voll-bracht! El - sa, mit
near. Call me, no harm, and straight the deed is done! El - sa, with

sf cresc. - - - ff

hastily forward.)   (In a terrible tone, to Ortrud and Frederick.)

wem verkehrst du da?   Zu - rück_____
whom do you con - verse?   A - way_____

mf   cresc. - - -   ff

___ von ihr, Ver - fluch - te!   Dass nie__ mein Au - ge
from her, ac - cursed ones!   And nev - er let my

Hns.   Wind.   ff

(Frederick makes a gesture
of pain and rage.)

je euch wie - der bei ihr seh'!
eyes See you a - gain with her!

Str.   più f

(Lohengrin turns towards Elsa, who, as he
calls her name, sinks overwhelmed at his feet.)   Più moderato.

molto espress.   El - sa, er - he - be dich! In
El - sa, get up,__ my love! With-

ff rit.   dim.   più p

(she sinks upon his breast.)

Lohengrin.

lento.

(Lohengrin solemnly conducts Elsa past the nobles, to the King.)

steh'n!   Heil dir, El - sa!   Nun___ lass vor Gott___ uns gehn!
own!   Come then, El - sa!   Come,___ in the sight___ of God!

The Ladies and Pages.

Heil! Heil!
Hail! Hail!

Heil! Heil!   Heil!
Hail! Hail!   Hail!

(in enthusiastic emotion.)

The Men.

Seht, er ist von Gott ge - sandt!
See, this man was sent from God!

lento.

p Org.

Wind.

(As Lohengrin passes with Elsa, the men deferentially make way.)

The Men.

TENOR I.

TENOR II.

Heil   El - sa von Bra-
Hail,   El - sa of Bra-

BASS I.

BASS II.

Heil, Heil euch!
Hail, to___ you!

(Conducted by the King, Lohengrin and
Elsa slowly approach the Minster.)

Heil dir, El-sa!
Hail to El-sa!

bant!
bant!

Ge-seg-net sollst du
Most bless-ed are your

Ge-seg-net sollst du schrei-ten!
Most bless-ed are your foot-steps!

The Ladies and Pages.

SOPRANO.

Heil
Hail

ALTO.

Heil dir,
Hail, most

Ge-seg-net sollst du schrei-ten!
Most bless-ed are your foot-steps!

Heil dir,
Hail, most

schrei-ten!
foot-steps!

Heil dir!
Hail, oh hail,

Heil dir,
Hail, most

Heil dir,
Hail most

Gott mö-ge dich ge-
May God di-rect your

sa von Bra-bant! Heil_____ dir!
sa of Bra-bant! Hail!_____ Hail!

sa von Bra-bant! Heil_____ dir!
sa of Bra-bant! Hail!_____ Hail!

TENOR I. II.

sa von Bra-bant! Heil_____ dir!
sa of Bra-bant! Hail!_____ Hail!

BASS I. II.

sa von Bra-bant! Heil_____ dir!
sa of Bra-bant! Hail!_____ Hail!

(Here the King, with the bridal pair, has reached the highest step of the Minster; Elsa with deep emotion turns to Lohengrin, who clasps her in his arms. From this embrace she looks up with a startled expression, and at the foot of the steps *R. H.* perceives Ortrud, who lifts an arm against her with an expression of certain triumph; Elsa, terrified, turns away her face.)

(As Elsa and Lohengrin, conducted by the King,

proceed to the entrance of the Minster, the curtain falls.)

End of the Second Act.

Act III.

Introduction.

3 Flutes, 3 Oboes, 3 Cls. in A, 3 Bassoons, Horns in G, 3 Trumpets in C, 3 Trombones, Tuba, Kettle-drums in G & D, Triangle, Cymbals, Tambourine & Strings.

D. Bass Trombs.
Hns. & Bssn.

(The curtain rises.)

Scene I.

(The bridal chamber; to the right, an oriel casement, which is open. Music behind the stage, at first heard quite in the distance, and gradually approaching nearer; at the middle of the strain, doors at the back of the stage *R.* and *L.* are opened; the Ladies enter *R. H.* leading in Elsa, the King and Nobles leading in Lohengrin; Pages with lights go before them.)

On the stage. *3 Flutes, 2 Oboes, 2 Cls. in B, 2 Bassoons, Horns in B flat & E flat, 2 Trumpets in B flat, Triangle & Harp.*

In the Orchestra. *(Same score except Triangle, Cymbals & Tambourine, with Harp added.)*

Eight Ladies. (after they have gone round once.)

FOUR SOPRANOS.

(When the two trains meet in the centre of the stage, the Ladies lead Elsa to Lohengrin, who embrace, and remain thus standing in the centre. Eight Ladies walk in slow procession round Lohengrin and Elsa, while these are divested of their heavy upper garments by the Pages.)

FOUR ALTOS.

Wie Gott euch
As God has

se - lig weih - te, zu Freu - den weih'n euch wir;
giv - en you bless-ings, We joy to bless you, too.

(They go round a second time.)

Lie- bes- glück's Ge- lei - te denkt lang— der Stun - de hier!
joys to come re- mem- ber This bow— - er blest for two!

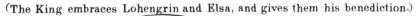

(The King embraces Lohengrin and Elsa, and gives them his benediction.)

(The Pages give a signal to retire; the two trains resume the order in which they entered. During the following, all pass before the bridal pair, the men going out *R. H.,* the ladies *L. H.*)

Tempo I.

In Orchestra.

Wind on the stage.

All the Nobles and Ladies.

Treulich bewacht blei-bet zu-rück, wo euch der Se - gen der Lie - be be-
Faith-ful-ly watched, rest in this place, Where there a-wait you the bless-ings of

Treulich bewacht blei-bet zu-rück, wo euch der Se - gen der Lie - be be-
Faith-ful-ly watched, rest in this place, Where there a-wait you the bless-ings of

Treulich bewacht blei-bet zu-rück, wo euch die Lie - be be-
Faith-ful-ly watched, rest in this place, Where there a-waits you all

Hp. & Wind.

wahr'! Sieg-reicher Muth, Min-ne und Glück eint euch in Treu-e zum
love! Val-or-ous might, ra-di-ant grace, Now are u-nit-ed by

wahr'! Sieg-reicher Muth, Min-ne und Glück eint euch in Treu-e zum
love! Val-or-ous might, ra-di-ant grace, Now are u-nit-ed by

se - lig-sten Paar. Strei-ter der Tu-gend, blei-be da-heim!
heav-en a-bove. Cham-pion of vir-tue, here you will stay,

1st TENOR.

se-lig-sten Paar. Strei-ter der Tu-gend, blei-be da-heim!
heav-en a-bove. Cham-pion of vir-tue, here you will stay,

1st & 2nd TENORS.

blei-be da-heim!
here you will stay,

nahm euch nun auf, dem Glan- ze ent- rückt.
Splen- dor and pomp must now be shut out.

nahm euch nun auf, dem Glan- ze ent- rückt.
Splen- dor and pomp must now be shut out.

nahm euch nun auf, dem Glan- ze ent- rückt.
Splen- dor and pomp must now be shut out.

(Here both trains have passed entirely off the stage; the last pages that close the procession shut the doors.)

Gradually receding.

Treu- lich be- wacht bleibet zu- rück,
Faith- ful- ly watched, rest in this place,

Treu- lich be- wacht bleibet zu- rück,
Faith- ful- ly watched, rest in this place,

Treu- lich be- wacht bleibet zu- rück,
Faith- ful- ly watched, rest in this place,

wo euch der Se- gen der Lie- be be-
Where there a- wait you the bless- ings of

wo euch der Se- gen der Lie- be be-
Where there a- wait you the bless- ings of

wo euch der Lie- be be-
Where there a- waits you all

(When the procession has quitted the room, Elsa, overcome by emotion, sinks upon Lohengrin's breast. As the music dies away he seats himself on a couch by the oriel window, and draws Elsa gently towards him.)

Second Scene.
(Elsa and Lohengrin.)
(Same score as before, except Harp)

Molto tranquillo.

Lohengrin.

Das sü-sse Lied ver-hallt; wir sind al-lein, zum
The bliss-ful song has ceased; we are a-lone, The

er-sten Mal al-lein, seit wir uns sah'n. Nun sol-len
first and on-ly time since first we met. Now have we

wir der Welt ent-ron-nen sein, kein Lauscher darf des Her-zens
put the world a world a-way. No lis-t'ner hears the greet-ings

Grü-ssen nah'n. El-sa, mein Weib! Du
from our hearts. El-sa, my wife: my

sü-sse, rei-ne Braut! Ob glück-lich du, das sei mir jetzt ver-
sweet, my maid-en bride! And are you hap-py, now that you are

Poco più animato.

Gott ver - leiht, die nur Gott _____ ver - leiht!
God be - stows, on - ly God _____ be - stows!

Gott ver - leiht, die nur Gott _____ ver - leiht!
God be - stows, on - ly God _____ be - stows!

Poco più animato.

Lohengrin.

Wie hehr er-kenn' ich un-srer Lie - be
How won - drous is the love that now u -

We - sen! Die nie sich sah'n, wir hat - ten uns ge - ahnt; _____ war
nites us! Be - fore we met we had di - vined that love. _____ The

ich zu deinem Streiter aus-er-le - sen, hat Lie - be mir zu dir den Weg ge-
choice was made that I should be your cham-pion, But love it was that showed the way to

ich vor dei-nem Blick zer-flie-ssen, gleich ei-nem Bach um-win-den dei-nen
woke a wish to melt be-fore you, And like a brook to wind a-bout your

Schritt, als ei-ne Blu-me, duftend auf der Wie-sen, wollt' ich ent-
path; Or like a flow-er, mak-ing mead-ow fra-grant, So did I

zückt mich beugen deinem Tritt. Ist dies nur Lie-be?— Wie soll ich es
wish to bow be-neath your step. Is this what love is? How shall I de-

nen-nen, dies Wort, so un-aus-sprechlich wonne-voll, wie, ach! dein Na-me, den ich
scribe it, This word that tells of joy be-yond mere words, Or like your name, ah, which I

Lohengrin.
(caressingly)

nie darf ken-nen, bei dem ich nie mein Höch-stes nen-nen soll! El-sa!
may not ut-ter, With which I can-not name my high-est known? El-sa!

Elsa. *(lingering over her words.)*

Wie süss mein Na-me deinem Mund' ent-gleitet! Gönnst du des dei-nen holden Klang mir
How sweet my name sounds when I hear you say it! Why do you grudge the gra-cious sound of

nicht? Nur, wenn zur Lie-bes-stil-le wir ge-lei-tet, sollst du ge-
yours? On-ly when love in still-ness holds us close-ly, You must al-

stat-ten, dass mein Mund ihn spricht. Ein-sam, wenn Niemand wacht; nie sei der
low my mouth to speak your name. Soft-ly, when no-one wakes; Nev-er in

Lohengrin.

Mein süsses Weib!
O my sweet wife!

Moderato mosso.

Welt er zu Ge-hör ge-bracht! *(Lohengrin tenderly embraces Elsa, and points through*
hear-ing of the world out-side.

Wood.

Lohengrin.

the open casement to
the flower-garden.)
Ath-mest du nicht mit mir die sü-ssen Düf-te?
Say, do you breathe, as I, the sweet a-ro-ma?

Str. con sordini.

simile.

Cello.

O _ wie so hold be-rau-schen sie den Sinn! Ge-heim-niss-voll sie
Oh, how its o-dor rav-ish-es the sense! Mys-ter-ious-ly it

na-hen durch die Lüf-te,_ frag-los __ geb' ih-rem Zau - ber ich mich
brings to us its fra-grance Ques-tion-less do I let ___ its mag-ic

(raising his voice.)

hin. So ist der Zauber,der mich dir ver - bun-den, da als ich zu-
bless. Such is the mag-ic that has bound me to you, On that first of

erst, du Sü-sse, dich er - sah; nicht dei-ne Art ich
days, O sweet one,when we met. No need to ask you

brauch-te zu er - kun-den, dich sah mein Aug',_ mein Herz be-griff dich
whence you were de - scend-ed: Eyes knew the truth, and heart did un - der-

da. | Wie mir die Düf - te hold den Sinn be -
stand. | And as this fra - grance gent - ly takes my

rü - cken, nah'n sie mir gleich aus räth - sel-vol - ler
sens - es, Waft - ed to me by e - nig-mat - ic

(with ardor)
Nacht, so dei - ne Rei - ne muss - te mich ent -
night, E - ven that way your pu - ri - ty en -

zü - cken, traf ich dich auch in
thralled me, Though heav - y slan - der

(Elsa conceals her confusion by clinging devotedly to Lohengrin.)

schwerer Schuld Ver - dacht.
tried to hide your worth.

Elsa.

Ach! könnt' ich dei-ner werth er-schei-nen! Müsst' ich vor
Ah, could I prove that I am wor-thy, Not seem like

dir nicht___ bloss ver-geh'n! Könnt' ein Verdienst mich dir ver-
noth-ing___ in your eyes! Could I per-form some deed to

ei-nen, dürft' ich in Pein für dich mich seh'n! Wie
lift me, Could I en-dure some pain for you! And

du mich traf'st vor schwe-rer Kla-ge, o! wüss-te ich auch dich in
as you found me crushed with sor-row,Could I but save you too from

Noth! Dass muth-voll ich ein Mü - hen
ills! That brave - ly I might bear some

Slower. **Lohengrin** (sternly and gravely, stepping

mich sei Schweigens Kraft be-währt!
me can si-lence' strength be proved.

Höch-stes Vertrau'n hast
Great-est of trust al-

back a few paces.)

du mir schon zu dan-ken, da deinem Schwur ich Glau-ben gern gewährt;
read-y has been shown you, For I placed full-est faith up-on your oath.

wirst nimmer du vor dem Ge-bo-te wanken, hoch ü-ber al-le
If you will nev-er break the oath you swore me, Then of all wom-en

(He quickly turns again fondly

Frau'n dünkst du mich werth!
you will be the peer! *Molto più vivo.*

towards Elsa.)

An meine Brust, du Sü-sse, Rei-ne!
Come to my breast, you sweet and pure one!

Lohengrin. Nie soll dein Reiz ent - schwinden, bleibst du von
Nev - er your charms will less - en If you keep

Zwei - fel rein! Ach! Dich an mich zu bin - den, wie sollt' ich mäch-tig
free from doubt! How can I bind you to me: What pow-er do I

Elsa.

sein? Voll Zau - - ber ist dein We - - sen,
own? Your na - - ture is of mag - - ic,

durch Wun - - der kamst du her:
And mag - - ic brought you here.

wie sollt' ich da ge - ne - sen?
What is my fate there-af - ter,

Elsa.

Nichts kann mir Ru - he ge - ben, dem Wahn___ mich nicht ent -
No, I can-not be peace-ful, And noth - - ing gives them

reisst, als___ gelt' es auch mein Le - ben! zu
rest, But, though my life be for - feit, The

ff Wind.

wis - sen, wer du sei'st! Un - se - lig hol - der
know-ledge who you are. Un - can-ny, gra - cious

Lohengrin.

f Str. *ff Wind.* *dim.* *p*

El - sa, was willst du wa - gen?
El - sa, why do you dare this?

Mann, hör'! was ich dich muss fra - gen! Den Na - men sag' mir an! Wo -
man, Hear what I now must ask you: The name___ you tru - ly bear . . . From

Halt' ein!
For-bear!

Tnr., 'Cello, Bssn., & Hns.

El - sa, mei - ne sü - sse Frau! Dort will ich Ant-wort ihr be-
tire her as my love- - ly bride. There will her an-swer be made

rei - ten, dass sie des Gat - ten Art er - schau'!
read - y, So she may learn her hus - band's state.

(He departs,

sadly and solemnly. The Ladies lead out Elsa, who is speechless, *L. H.*)

(The day has slowly begun to dawn, the tapers are extinguished.)

(A large curtain closes over the front, hid-
ing the stage entirely from view.)

(On the stage.)

4 Tpts. (as though heard from the courtyard.) ff

(lunga.)

(On the stage.)

Third Scene.

In the Orchestra.— *3 Flutes, 3 Oboes, 3 Clarinets in B flat, 3 Bassoons, Horns in E flat, 3 Trumpets in C, 3 Trombones, Tuba, 3 Kettle-drums, Strings.*

On the Stage.— *2 Trumpets in E flat, 2 in F, 2 in D, 2 in E, 4 in C, Side-drums.*

(When the curtain is drawn aside, the scene presents the meadow on the bank of the Scheldt, as in the first Act; a brilliant dawn gradually brightens into full daylight.)

(A Count with his train of vassals enters *R. H.*; he steps from his horse, which he gives in charge to an Esquire; two Pages bring his shield and spear. He sets up his banner, round which the vassals group themselves.)

Tpts. in D on the stage (approaching rapidly from *R. H.*)

(nearer and louder.)

cresc. poco a poco.

(Whilst a second

Count enters after the same manner as the first, the trumpets of a third are heard approaching.)
Tpts. in F (from a distance, coming nearer.)

più f

(nearer and louder.)

cresc. poco a poco.

(A third Count enters in the same fashion with his vassals. Each band gathering round its ban-

ff Wind in Orchestra.

296

ner, the Counts and Nobles salute each other, examine and praise each others arms, etc.)

Tpts. in E on the stage (advancing from the background *R. H.*)

(nearer and louder.)

cresc. poco a poco -

(A fourth Count enters with his train *R. H.*, and takes up his stand in the centre at the back. When
Tpts. of the King in C.

the trumpets of the King are sounded, all group themselves in order and unfurl their banners.)

Chorus. All the Men. (striking on their shields as the King reaches the oak.)

Heil,_____ Kö - nig Hein - rich!
Hail,_____ hail, King Hen - ry!

Kö - nig Hein - rich Heil!_____
Hail, King Hen - ry, hail!_____

On the stage.
Tpts. of the King.

All the Tpts. on the stage.

Side Drums (on the stage)

Tpts. in Orch.

The King.

Habt Dank, ihr Lie - ben von Bra - bant!
Have thanks, good liege men of Bra - bant!

Wie fühl' ich stolz mein Herz ent - brannt, find' ich in je - dem deut - schen
Now is my heart a - glow with pride! May I, in ev - ry Ger - man

Land so kräf-tig rei-chen Heer-ver-band! Nun soll des
land Find such a strong and val - iant band! Now let the

Rei - ches Feind sich nah'n, wir wol-len ta - - pfer ihn em -
king - dom's foe ap - pear, We'll take him on, we'll meet him

The Four Nobles.

Lento.

So will's der Schützer von Brabant: wer die-ser ist, macht er be - kannt.
So wills the Guard-ian of Bra-bant. The man we bear he'll soon make known.

Lento.

Ob. & Cl.

Wood. p

(Elsa, with a numerous train of Ladies, enters, and comes forward with slow and faltering steps.)

The Men.
(in two Choruses.)

1st Chorus.

Seht, El - sa naht, die Tugend - rei-che!
Look, El - sa comes, most rich in vir -tue.

Fl. & Ob.

(The King goes to meet Elsa, and leads her to a seat opposite to the oak.)

2nd Chorus.

Wie ist ihr Ant - litz trüb' und blei - che!
Her coun-te-nance is pale and trou-bled.

'Cello.

The King.

Wie muss ich dich so trau - rig seh'n! Will dir so nah' die Trennung geh'n?
Why must I see you look so sad? Do you find part-ing hard to make?

Str. p

Wood.

dim. p

(Elsa tries to look up at him, but cannot.)

A Portion of the Chorus. (at the back.)

Vivo.

(Great stir

Macht Platz,   macht
Make way,   make

Vivo.

Str.

in the background.)

Platz   dem   Hel — — den von Bra — bant!
way,   the   Guard — — ian of Bra — bant!

cresc.

Ped.

All the Chorus.

(Lohengrin, fully armed, as in Act I, enters and strides solemnly and gravely to the front.)

Heil!
Hail!

Heil   dem   Hel — den   von   Bra —
Hail   the   Guard-ian   of   Bra —

Tutti. ff

Ped.

Ped.

Heil   dem Hel — den   von   Bra — bant!   Heil!
Hail   the Guard-ian   of   Bra — bant!   Hail!

bant,   dem Hel — den   von   Bra — bant!   Heil!
bant,   the Guard-ian   of   Bra — bant!   Hail!

Ped.

304

45611

Chorus. All the Men.

Wir har-ren dein in Strei-tes Lust, von
We wait for you to give the word And

dir ge-führt, des Sieg's be-wusst.
lead them forth with con-q'ring sword.

Lohengrin. **Più moderato.**

Mein Herr und Kö-nig, lass dir mel-den:
My lord and sov'-reign, be en-light-ened:

Str. Tpts. & Tromhs.

die ich be-rief, die küh-nen Hel-den, zum Streit sie füh-ren darf ich
They whom I called, these dough-ty he-roes, I dare not sum-mon to the

bin?
am.
Nun hat sie ih-ren theuren Schwur ge-brochen, treu-lo-sem
Now, bro-ken is that sa-cred oath' she swore to: Treach-er-ous
Wind.

(all express the utmost agitation.)

Rath gab sie ihr Herz da - hin! Zu
coun - sel made her yield her heart. To

loh - nen ih-res Zweifels wil - dem Fra-gen, sei nun die Antwort län - ger nicht ge-
sat - is -fy her prod-ding wild sus - pi - cions No long-er shall that an - swer be with-

spart; des Fein-des Drängen durft' ich sie ver-sagen; nun muss ich
held. And though I need not heed an ur-gent foe-man, Yet must I

Con moto moderato.
(his face gradually becomes transfigured.)

kün-den,wie mein Nam' und Art! Jetzt merket wohl, ob ich den Tag muss
now re-veal my name and birth. Now mark me well, and ask if I fear

Gral zu dienen ist er - ko - ren, den rü - stet er mit ü - ber-ir-discher
cho - sen for the Grail's at - tend-ance Is armed there-with with more than mor-tal

Macht: an dem ist je - des Bö - sen Trug ver - lo - ren. wenn
might. No e - vil pow'r can ev - er o - ver-throw him. To

ihn er er-sieht, weicht dem des To - des Nacht. Selbst wer von ihm in fer - ne
look on the Grail de - stroys the dream of death; And if one such is sent to

Land' entsendet, zum Strei-ter für der Tugend Recht er-nannt. dem wird nicht sei - ne
dis-tant re-gions When called to be the cham-pi-on of right, E - ven here will the

heil' - ge Kraft ent-wendet. bleibt als sein Rit - ter dort er un - er - kannt: so
ho - ly pow - er serve him.While he's un-known he's mas-ter of the spell. Of

heh - rer Art doch ist des Gra - les Se - gen, ent - hüllt, muss er des Lai - en Au - ge
such high source though is the ves - sel's bless-ing Re - vealed, straight will it flee the lay - man's

fliehn: _ des Rit - ters drum sollt Zweifel ihr nicht he - gen, erkennt ihr ihn, dann muss er
eye. And so its knight must nev-er be sus - pect-ed, For if once known, then must he

von euch ziehn. _ Nun hört, wie ich ver - bot'-ner Fra - ge
leave the land. Now hear how I must an - swer what was

loh - ne! Vom Gral ward ich zu euch da-her ge-sandt; mein Va - ter Par-zi-val
asked me. The ho - ly Grail has sent me here to you. My fa-ther Par-si-fal

trägt sei - ne Kro - ne. sein Rit - ter ich _ bin Lo-hengrin ge-nannt.
rules in my coun-try. His knight am I and Lo-hen-grin my name.

45611

Elsa (crushed.)

heil' - gen Won - ne - zäh - ren!
eyes pour joy - ful tear - drops.

Mir schwankt der
The floor is

heil'- gen Won - ne - zäh - ren!
eyes pour joy - ful tear-drops.

Aug' in Won - ne - zäh - ren!
eyes pour joy - ful tear - drops.

pp

brennt mein Aug' in heil'-gen Won - ne - zäh - ren!
made my scald - ing eyes pour joy - ful tear - drops.

più p

ge in Won - ne - zäh - ren!
ing with joy - ful tear - drops.

più p

Aug' in heil' - gen Won - ne - zäh - ren!
cheeks with hap - py ho - ly tear - drops.

più p

heil' - gen Won - ne - zäh - ren!
eyes pour joy - ful tear - drops.

più p

pp
K.Dr.

'Cello.

accel.

Bo - den! Wel-che Nacht! O Luft, Luft der Unglück - sel' - gen!
reel - ing! It is night! Oh, air, air for me most wretch-ed!

Tur. *cresc.* *Vlns.*

All the Str. *p molto cresc.*

(As she is falling, Lohengrin **Lohengrin.**
catches her in his arms.) Vl- *Vivo.* *più lento.* *Allegro, a tempo.*

Vl- O, El-sa! Was_hast du mir an-ge-than?
O *Wind.* El-sa! What is it you've done to me?

Str.

f *p* *f* *p*

Ped. * Ped. *

Als mei-ne Au-gen dich zu-erst___ er-sahn, zu dir fühlt'
When first my eyes were pleas-ured by___ your sight, I felt for___

___ ich in Lie-___-be mich entbrannt, und schnell hatt' ich ein neues
___ you a kin-___-dling fire of love, And straight-way did a joy up-

Glück er-kannt; die heh-re Macht, die Wunder meiner Art, die
lift my heart. The tow-ring might, the won-der of my state, The

Kraft, die mein Ge-heim-niss mir bewahrt, wollt'___ ich dem Dienst des reinsten
pow'r which with my se-cret is in-volved, These___ were to serve the pur-est

Herzens weih'n:___ was ris-sest du nun mein Geheimniss ein? Jetzt___ muss ich
heart a-live. Why did you wrest my se-cret from my breast? Now___ must I,

dan - nen! Des Füh - - rers har - ren dei - ne Man - nen!
help - less! Your men are wait - ing for their lead - er.

Man - nen, des Füh - rers har - ren dei - ne Man - nen! O bleib', und zieh' uns
lead - er. Your men are wait - ing for their lead - er. Oh stay, and do not

Des Füh - - rers har - ren dei - ne Man - nen! O bleib', und zieh' uns
Your men ___ are wait - ing for their lead - er. Oh stay, and do not

O bleib'! Zieh' uns nicht von dannen! Des Führers har - - ren dei - ne Man -
Oh stay, do not leave us help - less! your men are wait - - ing for their lead -

nicht von dan - nen! Des Füh - rers, des Führers har - ren dei - ne Man - - -
leave us help - less! They wait you, your men are wait - ing for their lead - - -

nicht von dan - nen! Des Füh - rers, ja, har - ren dei - ne Man - - -
leave us help - less! They wait you, your men wait for their lead - - -

Lohengrin. *Animato e vivo.*

nen! O Kö - nig, hör'! Ich darf dich nicht ge - lei - ten! Des Gra - les Rit - ter,
er. O king, at - tend! I dare not be their lead - er! The ho - ly ser - vant,

nen!
er.

nen!
er.

Str. *colla parte.*

ff *Wind.* *ff*

habt ihr ihn er-kannt,—wollt' er in Un-ge-hor-sam mit euch strei-ten,—
if he is but known, Would, if he broke his vows to help your bat-tles,

ihm wä-re al-le Man-nes-kraft ent-wandt! Doch, grosser
Lose all his god-like, man-ly strength and skill. Yet, might-y

Kö-nig! lass mich dir weis-sagen:— Dir Reinem ist ein gro-sser Sieg ver-
mon-arch, let me make pre-dic-tion: You, true-heart, have a vic-to-ry to

lieh'n! Nach Deutschland sol-len noch in fernsten Tagen, des
come, This land of yours shall nev-er feel the foot-tramp of

(general excitement.)

Ostens Hor-den siegreich nim — mer zieh'n!
East-ern hordes from now or times re-mote!

(She remains for a long time like
one petrified in the same position.)

Lohengrin (deeply moved.)

Ha! der Schwan!
Ha! The swan!

Schon sendet nach dem Säumigen der Gral!
Too long I've stayed: The Grail has sent for me.

Tpts. & Trombs.

(While all stand with strained attention, Lohengrin
advances to the bank and bends over the swan.)

Andante moderato.

Mein lie - ber
My trust - y

Schwan!   Ach, die - se letz - te,   traur' - ge Fahrt, wie gern hätt' ich sie   dir _ erspart!
swan!   This lat - est jour - ney   pains _ my heart. Oh, that it _ had been spared to you!

In ei - nem Jahr,   wenn dei - ne Zeit   im Dienst zu En - de soll - te geh'n,
With - in a year,   when time _ you spent In serv - ice should be at _ an end,

dann, durch des Gra - les Macht be - freit,   wollt' ich dich an - ders wie - der seh'n!
Freed through the Grail's most ho - ly _ pow'r,   I hoped to see you oth - er - wise!

(He returns to the front towards Elsa, with an outburst of anguish.)

Vivo.

p molto cresc. — ff Tutti.

El - sa! Nur ein Jahr____ an dei - ner Sei - te hätt' ich als
El - sa! Just a year____ with you, be - lov - ed, Then had I

Zeu - ge dei - nes Glücks er - sehnt!__ Dann kehr - te, se - lig in des
wit-nessed to your hap - pi - ness!__ You would have joyed to see that

ritard. più moderato.

Wind.

Andante moderato.
(all express extreme

Gral's Ge - lei - te, dein Bru - der wieder, den du todt ge - wähnt.
one so blest by the Grail, your broth-er, whom you fan - cied dead.

Str.

cresc.

astonishment.)

8-----

(during the following he hands his sword, horn and ring to Elsa.)

333

338

fahrt, wie sich die Göt- -ter rä- chen, von de- ren Huld_ ihr euch ge-
learn the way the gods _ take venge- ance, Up-on whose grace _ you turned your

Adagio. (She remains drawn up in an attitude of savage exultation and ecstasy.)

wandt!
backs!

(Lohengrin, standing on the bank, has heard all that Ortrud said, he now sinks on his knees in mute prayer. All eyes turn with anxious expectancy to him. The white dove of the Grail flies slowly down and hovers over the skiff, Lohengrin perceives it, and with a grateful look rises quickly, and loosens the chain from the swan, who immediately sinks. In its place Lohengrin raises Gottfried, a fair

Tutti.

boy in shining silver raiment, from the river, and places him on the bank.)

Lohengrin. *f*

Seht da den Her- zog von Bra- bant, zum Füh - rer sei er euch er -
Be- hold the rul- er of Bra- bant! Ac-cept_ him as your right-ful

Allegro.

nannt!
lord!

Tutti.

ff

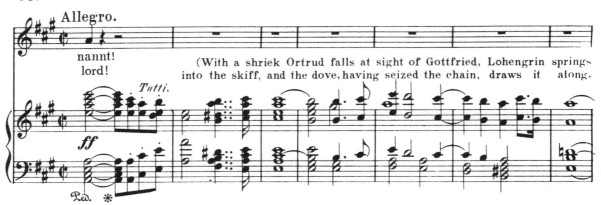

(With a shriek Ortrud falls at sight of Gottfried, Lohengrin springs into the skiff, and the dove, having seized the chain, draws it along.

Elsa, with a last look of joy, gazes on Gottfried, who advances to the King and makes his obeisance to him. All contemplate him with astonishment and joy, the Brabantians sinking on

their knees in homage. Gottfried rushes into Elsa's arms, who after a moment of joyous transport, turns her eyes again towards the river where Lohengrin has vanished.)

Elsa.

Mein Gat - te!   Mein Gat - te!
My hus - band!   My hus - band!

cresc.

(Lohengrin is seen once more in the distance. He stands with head bent, sorrowfully leaning on his shield in the skiff; at the sight of him all break into loud lamentation.)

(She sinks lifeless to the ground, supported by Gottfried.)

(As Lohengrin gradually recedes in the distance, the curtain falls.)

End of the Opera.